habitat explorer

River Explorer

Greg Pyers

Raintree

Chicago, Illinois

Printed and bound in China by Wing King Tong.

08 07 06 05 04
10 9 8 7 6 5 4 3 2 1

Library of Congress Cataloging-in-Publication Data:
Pyers, Greg.
  River explorer / Greg Pyers.
     p. cm. -- (Habitat explorer)
Summary: Takes an in-depth look at river habitats and the animals,
organisms, and plants that dwell there, as observed during an imaginary
journey down the Ganges River.
Includes bibliographical references (p.   ).
  ISBN 1-4109-0512-8 (lib. bdg. : hardcover)
  1-4109-0908-5 (paperback)
 1.   Stream ecology--Ganges River (India and Bangladesh)--Juvenile
literature. 2. Ganges River (India and Bangladesh)--Juvenile
literature. [1. Stream ecology. 2. Ganges River (India and Bangladesh)
3. Ecology.] I. Title. II. Series: Pyers, Greg. Habitat explorer.
  QH183.P97 2004
  577.6'4'09541--dc21
                                    2003009710

Editorial: Sandra Balonyi, Marta Segal Block, Carmel Heron
Design: Erica Barraca, Stella Vassiliou, Marta White
Photo research: Karen Forsythe, Wendy Duncan
Production: Sal d'Amico, Tracey Jarrett
Map: Guy Holt
Diagram: Nives Porcellato and Andy Craig

Acknowledgments
The publisher would like to thank the following for permission to reproduce photographs: p. 5 Getty Images/ National Geographic/Datta Berde; p. 6 N.G.Sharma; pp. 7, 12 Tom Brakefield; pp. 8, 9 (top & bottom), 19, 23 Wilderness Films India Ltd/Rupin Dang; pp. 10, 11 (background), 29 Getty Images/ National Geographic/Debal Sen; p. 11 Wolfgang Kaehler; p. 13 Getty Images/ National Geographic/Dinodia Photo Library; p. 14 Auscape/Erwin & Peggy Bauer; p. 15 AAP/Dirk Klynsmith; p. 16 Jeremy Horner; p. 17 Bio Images/Jason Edwards; p. 18 AP/AAP/Vikram Kumar; p. 20 Walker's Mammals of the World/G. Pilleri; p .22 APL-Corbis/Tiziana and Gianni Baldizzone; p. 24 Lonely Planet Images/ Lawrence Worcester; p. 25 Graham Robertson; p. 26 Getty Images/ National Geographic/Ashvin Mehta; p. 27 Neil Rabinowitz; p. 28 Roman Soumar.

Cover photograph of gharial reproduced with permission of Corbis/Michael & Patricia Fogden.

Disclaimer
All the Internet addresses (URLs) given in this book were valid at the time of going to press. However, due to the dynamic nature of the Internet, some addresses may have changed or ceased to exist since publication. While the author and publisher regret any inconvenience this may cause readers, no responsibility for any such changes can be accepted by either the author or the publisher.

Contents

Any words appearing in the main text in bold, **like this,** are explained in the Glossary.

The Himalayas

Imagine standing on a narrow, rocky path in a cold mountain valley. It is spring. Snow is melting, exposing the stony ground. Ahead is a huge, crumbling wall of dirty ice. This is the bottom end of a **glacier,** an ice river that is creeping downhill, tearing away rock and shaping the valley as it goes.

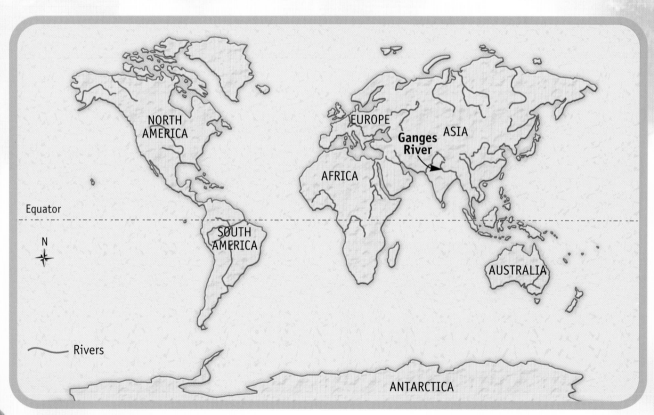

This map shows the locations of the world's largest rivers. The Ganges River flows from the Himalayan Mountains to Bangladesh.

There are cracks in the ice wall. A huge chunk breaks away and falls. It crashes into the stream gushing from beneath the glacier. You watch the stream flow through a narrow, rocky channel and on down the valley. This stream is the beginning of India's greatest river, the Ganges. And now you are going to follow it on its journey.

This glacier is where the Ganges River begins.

River habitats

Habitats are where animals and plants live. You will discover that, from its beginning in the mountains to its end at the sea, a river provides many habitats for animals and plants.

Explorer's notes

Beginning of a river:
- high mountains
- glacier
- narrow gully
- fast moving

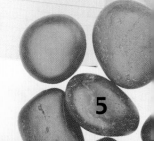

5

The Young Stream

The young stream moves through snow and rock. The water is crystal blue in the sunlight and emerald green in the shade. When it tumbles over rocks it becomes foamy white. These quickly moving parts of the stream are called **rapids.** A bird is diving into the water here. It is a dipper, hunting for worms, snails, and insects on the **streambed.**

Dipper adaptation

A dipper has special transparent eyelids that it closes underwater. These act like goggles to give the bird a clear view. Features like these eyelids are called **adaptations** because they help the dipper to survive.

The Ganges is just one of many fast-moving streams located high in the mountains.

A rare treat

You round a bend in the path and then stop—you see a snow leopard, an encounter that is a rare treat. It has not seen you. It has not heard you either, above the roar of the water. The snow leopard's thick fur has a color and pattern that make it almost invisible against the snow and rock. This is called **camouflage.**

The snow leopard's broad feet keep it from sinking into deep snow.

Explorer's notes

Snow leopard adaptations:
- thick fur to keep warm
- long tail for balance
- claws to catch **prey**
- colored and patterned fur for camouflage

The River Forms

The stream is joined by other streams and becomes a river. The current is strong and fast. Someone is hauling a huge fish from the water. It is a goonch, a type of catfish. Like other catfish, the goonch has barbels, or feelers, around its mouth that help it to find **prey.**

Before the Ganges reaches the plains, it has become a deep, wide, and fast-flowing river.

Dependency

The animals and plants of a **habitat** depend on each other in many ways. For example, catfish feed on the shrimps, worms, and shellfish that live on the streambed. Gorals use the pine trees for shade, and many birds build their nests among the branches.

Low rainfall

The river is flowing through steep, hilly country. Rainfall is low at this end of the Ganges. Chir pines can survive dry periods, and so they are the dominant trees here.

A small herd of gorals watches from the far bank. These goatlike animals are able to eat the tough bushes and grasses that grow in this region.

Chir pines grow on the steep hillsides.

This goral is taking shelter from the midday heat in a riverside cave.

The Plain

Further downstream, the river has slowed. It is deeper and wider here. You have boarded a boat, which is carried by the current as the river winds blow slowly across a wide plain. Most of the land here has been cleared for farming. Only small patches of forest and **woodland** remain. And now, from among some tall trees, fifteen Asian elephants have appeared.

Explorer's notes

Animals that were once plentiful on the river plain:
- Indian rhinoceroses
- swamp deer
- Asian elephants
- tigers
- gaurs (wild cattle)

Big river fish

Big fish in the river include goonch, mahseer, catla, and rohu, all of which grow to 5 feet (1.5 meters) in length.

River visits

Since elephants have difficulty cooling down in hot weather, they visit the river daily to bathe. Such large animals also need plenty of living space. But with so many people living along the river, they often come into conflict with farmers. A herd of elephants can do a lot of damage to crops.

An elephant cools down in the Ganges River.

11

Crocodiles

The day is hot. The water is tempting, but a swim is out of the question because there are gharials here. Gharials are crocodiles, and they feed on fish. They wave their narrow snouts quickly underwater and grasp passing fish in their pointy teeth.

Explorer's notes

Gharial statistics:

- maximum length:
  20 feet (6 meters)

- eggs laid in a sandy hole

- average number of
  eggs laid: 40

- eats fish

Male gharials have lumps that look like pots at the ends of their snouts. This gives gharials their name—a ghara is a pot.

Another species of crocodile in the Ganges is the mugger. This broad-snouted crocodile digs burrows, or holes, in the riverbank to get shelter from very high and very low temperatures.

Egg thief

A mongoose has appeared on a sandbank on the far side of the river. It is digging for something. It reaches into its hole and drags out a gharial egg.

Mongooses feed on gharial eggs.

13

Wetlands

The boat has taken a short side trip and enters a vast swamp. The water surface of this **wetland** is hidden beneath a mass of lotus plants. These water lilies have roots in the mud and a long stem that reaches to the water's surface. The leaves have air spaces that make them float.

Fishing cats

Fishing cats live in the Ganges wetlands. They catch fish by scooping them from the water using their sharp claws. These cats also eat frogs, snakes, and rodents such as rats.

Birds of the wetland

Birds are everywhere, though you hear them rather than see them. In the dense reed beds, marsh warblers are calling. These birds stitch their nests securely to the reed stems with strips of reed leaf.

A jacana is walking across the lotus plants, hunting for water insects. This bird has exceptionally long toes that prevent it from sinking.

The jacana's long toes enable it to walk across the leaves of water plants.

Explorer's notes

Wetland birds:
- marsh warblers
- purple swamp hens
- jacanas
- river terns

15

Pollution

The river has taken you through many large towns and cities. People come to the river to swim, wash, and even drink. To the millions of people who live along its banks, the Ganges is a sacred river. But you can see that the river is not always respected. Along the way there are pipes that empty waste and garbage into the river. You have even seen dead cows floating downstream.

Pollution is not only unhealthy for people and wildlife—it is also ugly.

Trapping pollution

Wetlands such as swamps trap pollution before it can drain into rivers. This is why in some cities around the world, wetlands have been built to help clean up polluted rivers.

Wildlife

This pollution has serious effects on the river wildlife. **Invertebrates,** such as worms, insects, and shellfish, absorb the poisons as they feed. The poisons are passed onto fish when they eat these invertebrates, and then to otters, gharials, and dolphins, all of which eat fish. The numbers of these animals have fallen because of the pollution.

Asian small-clawed otters need clean water so that they can see their fish prey.

Explorer's notes

Animals threatened by pollution:
- gharials
- Indian otters
- Asian small-clawed otters
- Ganges River dolphins

Floods

You are now within 310 miles (500 kilometers) of the sea. The weather has been pleasant and dry. But by the end of June, strong winds arrive from the Bay of Bengal, bringing with them the first storms of the monsoon season. These storms continue until October. So much rain falls that the Ganges often breaks its banks and floods the surrounding plain for many miles.

Smooth watersnake

The smooth watersnake has **adaptations** that help it survive in floods. It has smooth scales for slipping through the water and chasing its **prey** of frogs and fish. This snake even gives birth to live young underwater.

This is the flooded Ganges during monsoon season.

Stranded wildlife

While birds and bats escape the floods, animals that cannot fly may drown. If they are lucky, swamp deer, gaurs, sloth bears, and four-horned antelopes may become stranded on temporary islands. But, if the flooding lasts, these animals may run out of food and starve to death.

These Sambar deer are grazing on flooded plains.

Dolphins

The water has become very murky from the **silt** picked up by the river over its long journey. The pollution added to the river from towns, cities, and farms has only added to the murkiness. And then you see something you would never expect to see living in such dark depths: a dolphin.

The Ganges River dolphin is rarely seen.

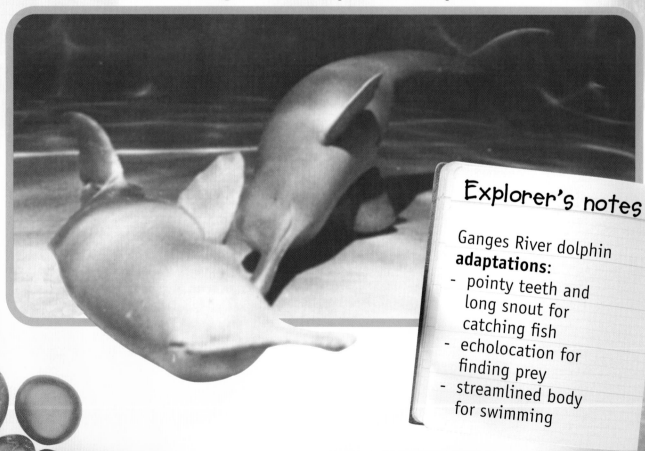

Explorer's notes

Ganges River dolphin **adaptations:**
- pointy teeth and long snout for catching fish
- echolocation for finding prey
- streamlined body for swimming

It was only for a moment, but the blow-hole was unmistakable. It opened to take a breath and then the animal was gone, back to the bottom to hunt for fish and **crustaceans.**

This dolphin was not a typical dolphin; it was a Ganges River dolphin. The murky water is no problem to this animal. In fact, with no lenses in its tiny eyes, this dolphin is blind. It finds its **prey** by **echolocation.**

Echolocation

Ganges River dolphins direct high-pitched sounds into the water. When these strike an object, such as a fish, the sounds bounce back. The dolphin hears these echoes and knows where its prey is. This is known as echolocation (locating by echo).

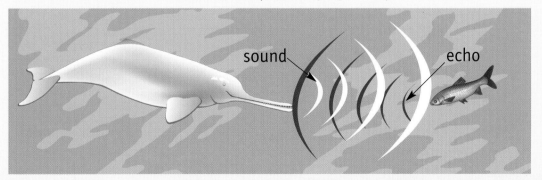

sound

echo

Delta

The river has slowed. Here, the mud and sand it is carrying sink to the bottom. Over thousands of years, so much mud and sand has built up that new land has formed. This land has blocked the river, and the water has had to find other ways to get through to the sea. And so, for the last part of its course, the Ganges becomes thousands of rivers flowing through a wide flat land called a **delta.**

Large deltas

The Mississippi River in the United States and the Nile River in Egypt have formed large deltas.

The Ganges Delta is so wide that boats are the best form of transportation.

Fertile land

The mud and sand deposited by the river are very **fertile.** This means that plants grow well in the delta. People have cleared the land to grow rice and other crops.

But many wild animals still live here. You can hear the calls of thousands of frogs. There are little grebes diving for tadpoles and fish. These birds have webbed feet and legs placed well back on their bodies so that they can propel themselves through the water.

A little grebe swims in the Ganges Delta.

Explorer's notes

Birds of the delta farmland:
- egrets
- house crows
- little grebes
- common mynas
- Indian pond herons

Swamp Forest

Further downstream, the water is beginning to become slightly salty. This is caused by water creeping in from the ocean. Small patches of forest grow here.

Hunting in the swamp forest

The boat stops. A chital (a kind of deer) is grazing in a clearing. Its spotted coat makes it difficult to see in the shadows and spots of light. It looks up...

The chital is also known as the spotted or axis deer.

In a side channel, the water is rippling. Something is swimming there. A tiger! It emerges onto the riverbank. Its stripes serve as **camouflage** and blend with the shadows of the trees. It settles and waits. The chital goes back to its grazing. The tiger edges forward, crouching, ears flat. The chital looks up but the tiger, the **predator,** is already charging. It reaches for the deer with claws extended and grasps the chital. With a single bite to the chital's neck, the tiger has its **prey.**

The Indian tiger will swim to reach its prey.

Explorer's notes

Predators of the swamp forest:
- Bengal tigers
- leopard cats
- Indian civets
- jungle cats
- fishing cats
- leopards

Mangrove Forest

The boat has left the main river channel and has entered a smaller stream that flows to the sea. The land is flat and covered by a very thick forest of small trees called mangroves. Seawater floods much of this land as tides roll in and out. The tide is out now and strange fish called mudskippers are moving around on the mudflats.

Obtaining oxygen

Living things need **oxygen** to survive. Because mangroves grow in waterlogged soil, which has no oxygen, their roots poke above the soil to absorb oxygen from the air.

Mudskippers

Mudskippers come out of the water to feed on worms and insects on the mudflats. They use their front fins to move. They breathe by holding water in their mouths and passing it over their gills. Every now and then they plunge their heads into the water to replenish their supply.

The mudskipper is a fish that can move around on land.

Journey's end

Your boat returns to the main channel of the river. The smell of the sea is in the air. The river has reached its end at the Bay of Bengal. Your journey is over.

Explorer's notes

End of a river:
- flat land
- wide plain
- slow moving

The River's Future

About 400 million people live on the Ganges River plain. Every day, more than 240 million gallons (900 million liters) of untreated sewage enters the Ganges. Factories add more pollution to the river. Many of the **habitats** along the river have been taken over for farming and cities.

Millions of people come to the Ganges to wash in its sacred waters.

Protecting the river

Despite the pollution and loss of habitat, there are areas along the river's length where wildlife is protected in national parks and reserves. The Sunderbans mangrove forests, for example, have been made a **World Heritage site.** This means that protecting these forests and their wildlife is important not just for India but for the whole world.

Return of the platypus

In Melbourne, Australia, platypuses have returned to rivers that were once too polluted for these animals to survive. Because people made sure not to pour poisonous waste down the drain, these rivers have been made clean enough for platypuses to survive.

People and wildlife live in harmony in the Sunderbans World Heritage site.

Find Out for Yourself

Visit a river near you. Observe the different kinds of **habitats** you see. Observe the animals and plants you see in these places. Observe the habitats at different times of the year to find out what changes occur.

Using the Internet

Explore the Internet to find out more about river habitats. Websites can change, so if the link below no longer works, don't worry. Use a kid-friendly search engine, such as www.yahooligans.com or www.internet4kids.com, and type in keywords such as "river animals," or even better, the name of a particular river or animal.

Website

http://www.slco.lib.ut.us/kidriver.htm
This website has many links to other websites for information about river habitats and wildlife around the world.

Books

Galko, Francine. *River Animals*. Chicago: Heinemann, 2002.

Gieseske, Ernestine. *River Plants*. Chicago: Heinemann, 2003.

Harrison, David L. Rivers: *Nature's Wondrous Waterways*. Honesdale, Penn.: Boyds Mills, 2003.

Glossary

adaptation feature of an animal or plant that helps it to survive

camouflage colors and patterns that help an animal to hide in its habitat

crustacean animal that has a hard, jointed shell (e.g., shrimp and crayfish)

delta broad, flat area formed by a river depositing sand and stone just before it reaches the sea

echolocation finding things by making sounds and listening for the echo

fertile having many nutrients

glacier river of ice that creeps slowly down a mountain valley

habitat place where an animal or a plant lives

invertebrate animal without a backbone (e.g., insect, worm, snail)

oxygen gas in the air that living things need to survive

predator animal that kills and eats other animals

prey animal that is killed and eaten by other animals

rapids steep and turbulent stretches of a stream

silt fine particles of sand and rock

streambed dried out place where a stream used to be

wetland habitat covered by freshwater

woodland habitat of trees growing well apart

World Heritage site place that the United Nations says should be preserved because it has special significance for all people

Index